TAL GH

Dyslexia

Althea

Illustrated by Frances Cony

Happy Cat Books

We have dyslexia, and we want you to know what it is like to have dyslexia. There are many kinds of dyslexia, but mainly it means that we have great difficulty in learning to read or write. Some people think dyslexia does not exist, and that those who say they have it are just lazy or stupid.

"Jo and Sarah were my best friends in nursery.
We started school together.

They were learning to read, but somehow I couldn't. I didn't understand why. When I tried to copy words, I didn't know what I was drawing, it didn't make sense. I couldn't read it. I didn't see how the shapes could have a meaning and I couldn't guess.

The teacher said I was lazy, mum and dad kept asking me to try harder. I got very upset, of course I wanted to read and write, I didn't want to be different.

I hated going to school. I started messing about and clowning around."

"Mum took me to see a psychologist who was really kind. She asked me lots of questions and she gave me word and number tests. Also I had to do funny things, like closing my eyes and touching my nose, then my left ear.

She told Mum that I have dyslexia. I'm not stupid or lazy. It's just that my brain works in a different way.

It's not your fault that reading and spelling are so difficult for you.

I needed help to learn. She told me that I was as bright as other children.

It was good to know I wasn't thick or stupid. I have extra lessons to help me. Mum or dad comes to my lessons, so they can learn to help me at home. I am left-handed, which makes it difficult to copy what the teacher does."

"When I'm thinking about something, I think in pictures and not in words. I can turn the pictures in my head and see them from all angles. Sarah says she mainly thinks in words, I expect that's why she's much better at writing than I am.

Dad has dyslexia. He's an engineer. He says he plans machines in his head, to see if they will work, before he draws them. Now he also uses a computer programme, which can turn objects round like the pictures in our heads."

"After we found out that I had dyslexia mum helped me. She taught me the names of the letters of the alphabet and the sounds they make. We made the big letters in play dough. I had an alphabet to copy, so I could put them in order. Now I am faster than dad in saying the alphabet!

Lower case letters are much more difficult to learn. We have them on the fridge, but I never know if they have slipped and turned upside down, or reversed themselves. It took me a very long time to be able to use them.

Now I can usually write the right letters, but my spelling is very bad. I have a spell check. It looks like a calculator. I also have a special dictionary, so I can try out new words."

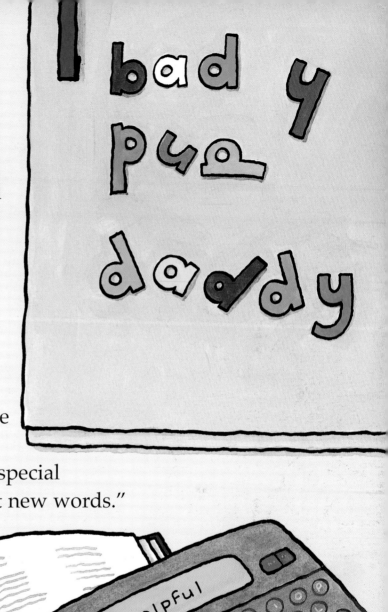

I write down the main idea, then think of all the things I could say about it. Then I should look the words up in my dictionary, so I don't make too many spelling mistakes. Then I have to work out what to say. My pet got too difficult to describe, so I drew a picture of it instead. Then I wrote about what it did."

Ben uses a laptop. it took him a while to learn the keyboard, but now it's easier than writing.

"History is fascinating," he says, "we are learning about the Anglo-Saxons. I'm writing about our museum visit. Now I can think about what I want to say, rather than worrying about how to keep the words on the line, or how to spell them."

Sometimes I get a word badly wrong and the spell check can't make head or tail of it.

Pippa says she still finds it very difficult to write things down.

"I love it when we have discussions, because I can join in, just like everyone else. I like answering questions, though sometimes I can't find the right word. I often find I know more than my friends do. I love drama too. I was in the school play last term. Mum helped me to learn my lines.

I like telling stories too. I can think of all sorts of exciting adventures. Sometimes I tell stories to a tape recorder, then other people can listen to them. If I try to write it down, I forget the story before I have finished. I have to think how to spell the words and how to keep the words on the line."

My teacher says I have lots of imagination.

Nobody realised that Guy had dyslexia, until his younger brother was tested. Everyone thought he was bright. "They kept telling me I was lazy.

Right, Guy. Remember what the story says...

I used to learn part of my reading book by heart, so my teacher thought I could read."

Guy says that after his dyslexia was diagnosed, he learnt to say 'I can't do that', without feeling bad about it.

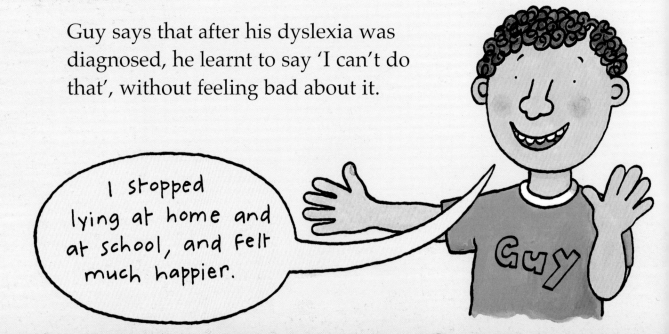

I stopped lying at home and at school, and felt much happier.

Roy used to hate reading. "When I look at the words on a page, both eyes see the words, but my brain makes the words

jump about and change size.

It's not just the letters, but the words, and the lines. It makes me feel sick and I can't read.

These green glasses help me, they stop the words from jumping about. The first time I wore them in school, I was told to take them off, because the teacher thought they were sunglasses."

Now the teachers know these glasses help me when I'm working.

When I'm r-e-a-d-i-n-g, I have to s-o-u-n-d out the w-o-r-d-s.

Guy says, "I can't take in the meaning of the stories at the same time.

Hello Guy. Here's Guy reading a story to you.

Sometimes I record myself reading aloud, then I listen to the story. Even better, I get books on tape and listen to other people reading them. My dad says, it's like when he reads in a foreign language. He can sound out the words, but he doesn't know what they mean."

"We have made a board game to help us with our spelling. Ben and Pippa come round to play too. It's like snakes and ladders, and you have to go back if you can't spell your word, but it's really good fun.

We have surprise cards, where you have to get up and do the hokey cokey, recite the days of the week, or walk round the room with a book balanced on your head!"

Nathan says that dyslexia can make life difficult in other ways too. "I can never remember what is going to happen next, or what day it is. Mum bought me a calendar for Christmas, and now I carry the slip for the day in my pocket."

Mum and I write on the back of it, to remind me what I have to do.

It's more difficult for me.

Lucy says, "I still can't tell the time, and I don't know my left from my right. I paint the little nail on my right hand red, to remind me which is my right hand.

When I'm crossing the road, I wait to see a car coming, so I know which way to look.

Now I'm old enough to go to the shop for mum. She writes a list of the things we need, as I won't be able to remember them by the time I get there."

I get scared when we go somewhere new, in case I get lost.

Lucy says that when she was younger, she even had to have a list if she went upstairs to do something. "Mum and I drew pictures to help me remember what I had to do.

Mum still makes me pack my books and things ready for school before I go to bed. We have a copy of my timetable in the kitchen. It helps me to remember to have my swimming things on the right day.

Monday	Tuesday		Thursday
	swimming		Music
GUIDES			
Friday	Satur...		
Art netball	dancing		

When I was younger, mum put my clothes on my chair in the right order, so I didn't put my trousers on before my pants!

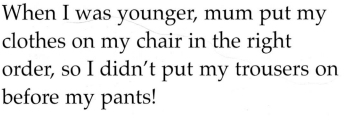

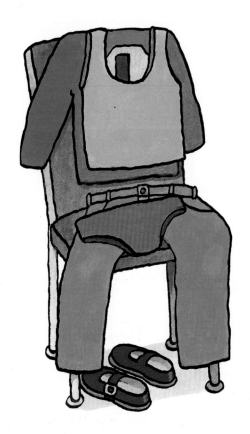

Maybe not!

My shoes were put side by side, so I didn't put them on the wrong feet."

"School is noisy and I find it hard to concentrate. I sit at the front in the classroom. When we have to copy from the board, it helps when the teacher numbers his lines, or does them in a different colour. Each time I look up to copy the next word I have to find it again.

Sometimes he rubs it off the board before I have time to write it down. When we have work to do at home the teacher writes a note in my homework book to remind me what to do."

When Lucy gets home, she is tired after trying to concentrate all day. "If it's a nice day I go for a walk or a bike ride to help me unwind. If the weather is bad, I watch a video. I don't think I'll ever be able to read long books, but I love watching plays and films."

I can't read the difficult words in our book on Dyslexia so Mum reads it to me.

"Sometimes when mum's upstairs, I have to answer the phone. I hate it. It's all right when it's gran, because I recognise her voice and we have a chat.

Sometimes it's to do with mum's work, and I can't write down messages. I ask their number and write it down, then read it back to them. I ask them how to spell their names.

I hate making phone calls too, because sometimes I press the wrong numbers, then I don't know what to say. Our new phone shows the number I have punched in, before it rings it, so I can check it very carefully."

Mum wants me to start making tea in an hour. This CD lasts an hour, so I will know when to get the food out.

The author would like to thank the Doza family,
the Hollick family, Jocelyn Hardwick, Jennifer Rye,
The British Dyslexia Association and the
William Westley Primary School for their
enormous help with this book.

HAPPY CAT BOOKS

Published by Happy Cat Books Ltd.
Bradfield, Essex CO11 2UT, UK

First published 2003
1 3 5 7 9 10 8 6 4 2

Text copyright © 2003, Althea Braithwaite
Illustrations copyright © 2003, Frances Cony
The moral rights of the author and illustrator have been asserted
All rights reserved

A CIP catalogue record for this book is available from the British Library

ISBN 1 903285 55 0 Paperback

Printed in Hong Kong by Wing King Tong Co. Ltd.